My heartfelt thanks
to my husband Hubertus for his support,
to Barbara Thomas, Gabriele von dem Hagen,
Christine Sawinski, Ilka Sampel, and my
Canadian friend Leona Niedzwiedz for their help,
to Franz-Eric and Christopher Schmidt
(my first test readers many years ago),
to my parents who have made so many things possible,
to Maximilian and Varena, because they give me so
much joy, and to my publishers Verlag an der ESTE
who have made my dream come true.

Doris Thomas

The author

Doris Thomas, born in 1966, first came into contact
with whales off the east coast of the USA in 1993.
Ever since she has been fascinated by these animals.
Doris Thomas tries to pass on her enthusiasm to
children with slide shows, lectures and her books.

Doris Thomas lives with her family in Pfaffenhofen,
Germany. "Zabu – The Adventures of a Young Orca" is
her first children's book; the German original is also
available. The sequel "Zabu – An Orca in Search of
the Unknown" has not been published in English yet.
The third part of Zabu's adventures in German will be
released soon.

For more information visit www.doris-t.de

Doris Thomas

Zabu
The Adventures of a Young Orca

Illustrated by Doris Thomas
Translated by Christine Sawinski

Verlag an der
ESTE

1st print of the English edition

© Verlag an der ESTE GmbH, Buxtehude 2008

Die deutsche Originalausgabe erschien unter dem Titel
„Zabu – Die Abenteuer eines jungen Schwertwals"

Umschlaggestaltung: Grafik-Design-Service
unter Verwendung der Bilder von Doris Thomas

Herstellung: Grafiche AZ, Verona

ISBN 978-3-86865-101-0

www.leseland.de

Contents

The Separation

The first day of Zabu's adventures started like a perfectly **ordinary*** day. In the morning nobody would have guessed that something unusual was about to happen.

Zabu was part of an **orca** family. He was not yet grown up, but neither was he a very young whale. His light patches shone brightly white and not yellowish-pink as in a baby whale.

Zabu was no longer fed by his mother, as he was able to catch his own fish. But there were many things he still had to learn. On that particular morning he was to make an **involuntary** start.

The sun was just rising and Zabu and his family were still quite sleepy. Orcas are very strong, and all animals of the sea are afraid of them. Therefore they were able to sleep peacefully and did not even need a guard.

* All words in bold are to be found in the Vocabulary on the pages 61 to 62.

The first sunbeams were just lighting up the sea when a shadow fell upon Zabu's family. The whales had heard the put-put of engines often before, but as they were still tired they did not take any notice of the small boat that was approaching them. Slowly and evenly something like a wall was lowered from the surface of the water to the bottom of the sea.

The boat moved closer and closer, **steered across** the whales and separated Zabu's family with a huge net.

Now the first few whales woke up and **roused** the rest of the family with cries of terror. "A net, a net," they shouted in confusion.

The whales took a frightened look around and realized what had happened. They were all on one side of the net except for Zabu. **Bewildered** he stared at the thing that separated him from his family.

"Zabu, stay where you are!" his mother shouted. Zabu could feel her fear and did not move. "What is this thing?" he asked. His mother tried to stay calm, even though she was very **agitated**.

"It is a net, Zabu. We have talked to you about human beings before. They don't live in the water, but they own boats, and with these nets they catch fish without going into the water themselves."

This was hard for Zabu to imagine. To catch fish with a silly thing like a net! Surely human beings must be slow swimmers and bad hunters. "But I can see you. Can't I just swim through the net?"

"No, Zabu, the net is too strong. You would get caught in it and might **suffocate**," his mother warned him. Zabu could not imagine this, but he had learned to listen to his mother. "But I want to be with you again. I want to be on your side. I don't want to stay here all alone."

Zabu was **sobbing**. The whales consulted with each other. They put their round heads together and all Zabu could see were their mighty **tail fins**.

Zabu's aunts also tried to figure out how to get Zabu over to their side. They had to be careful not to get too close to the net. Nets had become **death-traps** for too many animals before. Zabu was good at jumping, but in trying to cross the net he could easily **become entangled**.

Zabu became **impatient**. "Mummy! What can I do now?" he shouted desperately. In the meantime, his family had found a solution. "Well, Zabu, there is only one possibility. The safest way is the long way around the net."

Zabu stared. His mother continued: "The net is very long, and sometime the humans will pull it in one direction. By then we have to be far away, otherwise we will get caught."

Zabu tried to imagine what it would mean to be caught in a net. So far he had always been able to **surface** and **draw breath**. Caught in a net, he could not get to the surface anymore and would probably suffocate miserably.

Suddenly he realized the danger of the net and backed away with a strong movement of his **pectoral fins**.

"You want me to swim away from you, **give** the net **a wide berth** and then meet you again somewhere?" he asked and really knew the answer already. Yes, that was what he had to do.

He watched the sad and worried faces of his family. His mother tried to take away his fear and encouraged him. "Zabu, you are one of the strongest animals in the sea. No other animal will dare to attack you. You only have to beware of humans and stay away from them. Now go and don't worry, we will meet again soon."

Zabu did not want to worry his mother any further. He said good-bye bravely and with a heavy heart he turned his back on his family. With strong sweeps of his tail fin he started swimming towards his adventures.

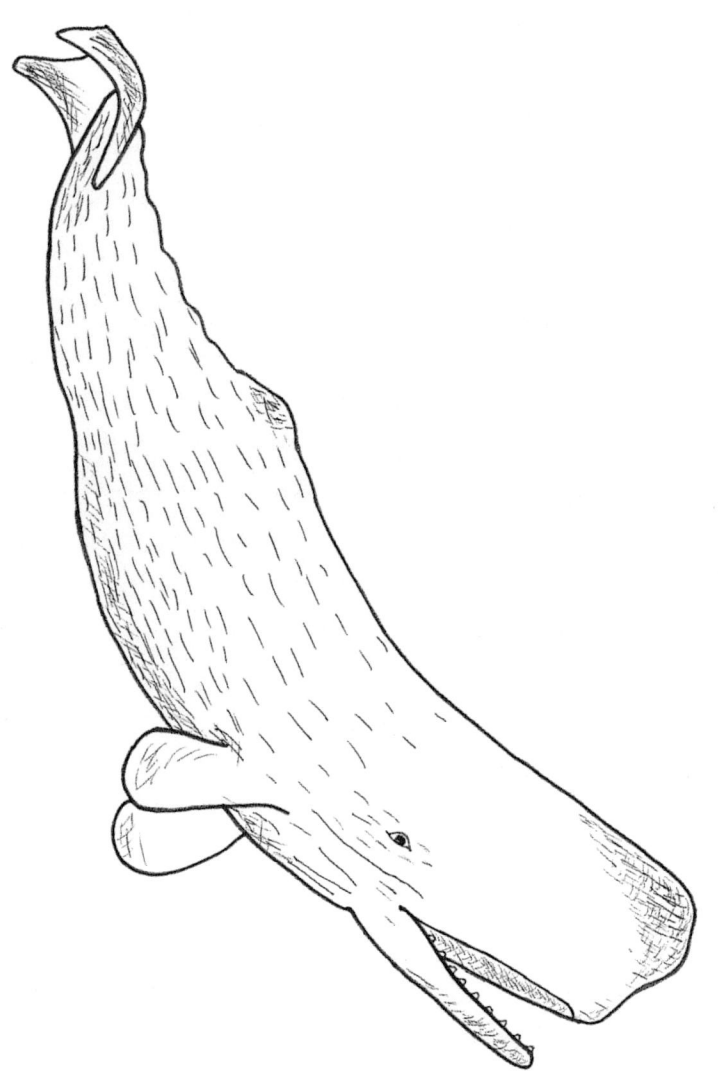

Fight with the Giant Octopus

For a while Zabu hurried because he hoped to be reunited with his family sooner this way. But after some time he became tired. The up-and-down movements of his tail fin became slower and slower and he decided to rest on the surface of the water for a moment.

He surfaced slowly and was welcomed by the sunbeams. "Well", he said to himself, quite satisfied, "really and truly I am quite well off. I can do what I want and perhaps I will find new friends. When I am with my family, all the other animals avoid us. They are afraid of our big mouths with the many teeth."

There are three different groups of orcas. Two of those eat fish. One of these groups live in the open sea and the other group, which Zabu belonged to, near the coast. The third group are fearful **predators**, because they hunt other **mammals** like **seals** and even whales.

Zabu was able to understand why all other sea animals were afraid of orcas. But he was very curious and would have loved to meet other species of whales as he found the stories he had heard about them quite unbelievable.

Zabu was lost in thought, but was brought back to reality quite suddenly by some noise. "Pooh!" he heard somebody breathing and saw a high **jet of water** shoot up in the air.

"Pooh!" Zabu heard again so noisily that he was frozen with fear. "Pooh, my little one, who are you?" The voice was so strong that Zabu stared with fright. An enormous head surfaced in front of him.

"Pooh, can't you speak?" Zabu **swallowed**. He plucked up courage.

"My, my, my... my name is Zabu," he stammered, "and who are you?" – "Pooh", said the big head, "my name is Pete."

Zabu was now able to identify the creature in front of him. "You are very big and you look very funny", he **marvelled**.

Pete's body looked very funny, indeed. His head was almost as big as the rest of his body. His eyes **were located** far back and his mouth was long and narrow. You could hardly see it from the front.

The big whale became impatient. He **was not used to being** examined this way. "Never seen a **sperm whale** before, have you?" he asked, and Zabu realized that he had been very impolite. "Sorry," he stammered, "**indeed**, I have never seen a sperm whale before. You must be very strong, aren't you?"

Pete was **flattered** and **boasted**: "Oh, yes. I am the biggest and strongest whale with teeth. There are bigger kinds of whales but they aren't fighters like I am. They are defenceless because they have no teeth and only eat very small animals. I eat giant **octopuses** with whom I fight at the bottom of the sea. Just look at my head."

He pushed out his head towards Zabu and showed him the many scratches and round scars.

Zabu could not understand how Pete had got these scars. "Did you get these fighting?", he asked **incredulously**.

"Yes," Pete answered proudly, "the round scars stem from the **suckers** of the octopuses. If you don't believe me, why don't you dive with me into the deep and I will catch us a **feast**."

For a short while Zabu hesitated, but then both whales gathered speed and took such a steep dive that for a moment only their tail fins could be seen above the water.

They dived deeper and deeper. It became darker and darker because the sunbeams could not penetrate the water to such depth.

"You'd better wait here for me," Pete **admonished** Zabu. "You cannot dive any deeper and it will be safer for you. You should watch me from here."

Zabu was quite happy with this suggestion, as he was starting to feel uncomfortable. He hung back while Pete dived further into the dark.

When he was no longer able to see the sperm whale clearly, Zabu discovered a second animal. Pete was making straight for it.

It was a giant octopus, a **squid**, bigger than any Zabu had ever seen before. Zabu counted ten tentacles. This monster had two tentacles more than the squid he knew!

"Oh gosh," he exclaimed. He would not have believed it possible. Pete opened his mouth wide and **pounced upon** his opponent.

The octopus extended two tentacles towards the sperm whale, whilst clinging to the ground with the remaining eight tentacles.

"If Pete can't free himself soon, he will suffocate," Zabu thought. Some of the suckers were already sticking to Pete's head but the fight was not yet settled. The whale turned around and kept snapping at the tentacles which loosened their grip on his head. With a strong sweep of his tail fin he made another attack.

Suddenly a dark cloud enveloped the fighters. Zabu held his breath. He could no longer see Pete and was very worried. By and by the inky cloud disappeared. Zabu could see a huge **shape**.

At first he could not see it clearly, but finally the picture became clearer. It was Pete. Zabu was relieved and greeted his friend with enthusiasm. "Wow, Pete. You really are a most brave and strong whale." Pete was exhausted, but he had remained the winner in this fight.

Proudly he held one of the gigantic tentacles in his mouth. "Come on, have a piece," he offered it to Zabu. When Zabu was full, Pete swallowed the rest in one piece. Together they surfaced and **recovered**. Pete from his exhausting fight and Zabu from the excitement.

When they were swimming next to each other and relaxing, Zabu remembered his family. He had managed to forget them for a while. "Sorry, but I have to leave you now, Pete," he sighed, "my family are waiting for me and I still have a long way to go."
Pete was full of understanding. "Perhaps we will meet again one day."

The two friends said good-bye, and the sperm whale showed Zabu the direction in which to swim. While Pete dived into the deep to look for new **prey**, Zabu started swimming towards his next adventure.

Taki's Birth

The sun had already gone past its highest point, it was afternoon. Zabu was happy. He had made friends with Pete who was very strong.

The sea was calm and Zabu kept jumping out of the water in high spirits.

Every time he fell back into the water there was a "Splash". He had great fun with his running jumps, "Woosh" and "Splash".

Again and again he jumped out of the water and slapped back onto the surface with his shimmering black-and-white body. Zabu kept doing this until he felt tired.

He was swimming just beneath the surface of the water when he heard some strange sounds. Surely they could have been heard for quite some time, but Zabu had been making so much noise that he never noticed.

Now he could hear quite a number of different sounds. They made up a song. Slightly scary, but beautiful. Zabu listened and tried to find out where this wonderful music was coming from. He made straight for it.

When the sun started tinting the sea red and the evening had come, Zabu could no longer **distinguish** where the sounds were coming from. He was surrounded by a beautiful song he had never heard before.

What kind of animal was able to produce such wonderful sounds? Zabu looked around. Yes, there was something there. A big whale was floating on the water. Zabu was curious and swam closer.

"Oh no, oh no, oh no," he heard a desperate voice. Zabu had a look at the big whale. Like Pete, this whale was much bigger than Zabu. It also looked completely different, even different from Pete.

Zabu especially noticed the long white pectoral fins. They were glowing under water. "Oh no, oh no," the **moaning** voice could be heard again. Zabu understood: Somebody was very frightened. "Hello?" he asked carefully. The big whale gave Zabu a scared look.

"Oh no, not an orca as well," Zabu heard him say. "Are you alone?" the big whale asked him.

"Yes, I am quite alone. I was separated from my family and now I am looking for them," Zabu explained. "Can I help you? You must be very unhappy because you are moaning so much." – "Yes, I am very worried. My name is Ulina and I am about to have a baby whale. Look!"

Zabu discovered a small tail fin underneath the lady whale's **belly**. "This is no reason to be unhappy," he said. The lady whale moaned: "I am looking forward to my baby, but it is in great danger." – "But why?" Zaby asked surprised, and Ulina tried to explain. She opened her big mouth.

Zabu could not believe his eyes, there where no teeth, only a lot of long, thin bones.

He remembered Pete's words: "Whales without teeth." Pete had also said that these whales were defenceless and no fighters in spite of their size.

The lady whale Ulina said: "I am a **humpback whale**. Our kind belongs to the species of **baleen whales**.

What you can see in my mouth is called baleen. I use them like a **sieve** to filter small crabs from the water.

Because I have no teeth, I cannot defend myself against enemies very well. Over there a big shark is just waiting to grab my baby. He will kill it because I cannot protect it."

Only then Zabu noticed the **shark**. He did not show any fear even though the shark was almost as big as himself. Bravely he positioned himself between Ulina and the shark.

"Don't be afraid, I will take care of the shark. Have your baby and don't worry!" Ulina was relieved and after a few minutes she pushed her newborn baby to the surface for its first breath of air.

Zabu had watched the birth with interest. But at the same time he kept an eye on the shark which was a good thing to do. At the last moment, Zabu was able to **intervene** when the shark tried to bypass him and grab the baby whale.

Zabu opened his mouth wide and swam towards the shark **at full tilt**. The shark seemed to understand that he had no chance of winning against an orca, turned around and disappeared as quickly as possible.

"Ha, ha, ha," Zabu laughed. **"That showed him."** He boasted a bit to impress mother and child.

Inside he felt a bit shaky because the shark had not exactly been small. Zabu was grateful that there had been no fight.

Finally he was able to greet the baby whale. "Hello you, what's your name?" – "I don't know," the little one replied in a squeaky voice. "Mummy, what's my name?"

Ulina thought about it. As a rule the **godmother**, who assists in the birth, chooses the name. This time none of her sisters had made it in time, and the only one who had helped her was Zabu, the orca.

"Well, what's to do?" she thought aloud. "I think it is only fair for Zabu to name you, my little son. Zabu, do you want to be his **godfather** and choose a name?" Zabu was full of enthusiasm and started thinking with all his might, which name would be suitable for such a sweet baby whale. "I feel very proud to be your godfather", he said to the young whale, "and you shall be called Taki from now on. Taki. That's your name."

The three whales started swimming next to each other relieved and satisfied, and Zabu learned a bit more about humpback whales. Diving, Ulina showed her **bent back** above the water surface, and Zabu understood, why this kind of whale was called "humpback whale".

He was able to imagine Ulina's fear when he learned how dangerous orcas can be for humpback whales. He explained straight away that he did not belong to this group of predators and only hunted fish. Zabu confirmed several times that he was harmless, and finally Ulina believed him. Zabu was **relieved**. Now he had two humpback whales as friends.

In the meantime, the sun had set and it had become quite dark. The sea was still filled with those beautiful songs, and Ulina explained that these songs were sung by the male humpback whales. "They want to impress us females," she said quietly. And even more quietly she added: "Isn't it lovely?"

The whole night long they listened to the male songs together. The next morning, they met Ulina's sisters and Zabu was able to say good-bye, because Ulina and Taki were now safe."

Just one more question. Can you tell me how to find my family?" Zabu was a bit disappointed when he did not get an exact answer, but they showed him the general direction, and then he was on his way.

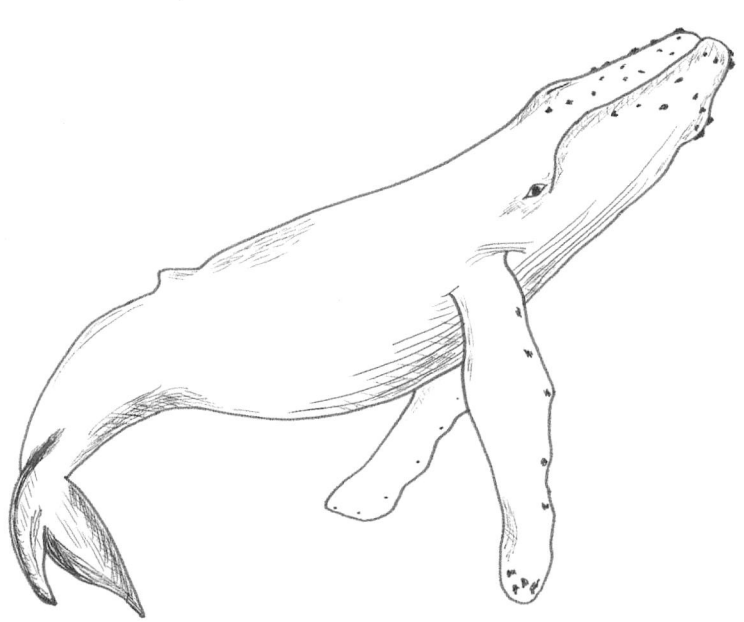

Makara, the Blue Whale

Zabu had already gone through a lot since the separation from his family. The adventure with Pete, when Zabu had watched the heavy fight with the giant octopus.

The **acquaintance** with Ulina and Taki, where he had shown courage and spirit. He had seen so many new things and his head was spinning with all the pictures of these experiences.

Zabu swam for many hours and was so deep in thought that he forgot his surroundings.

He hardly noticed what happened around him or what lay ahead of him in the water. He was roused from his daydreams none too gently when suddenly he was unable to swim any further. There was a big, lightly coloured wall suspended in front of him.

Zabu was amazed. Even though he seemed to have a rock in front of him, the huge wall gave signs of life.

Zabu could feel it quite clearly. This had to be an animal with warm blood in its **veins**, like himself. But all he could see was this strange wall which at second glance had a blue **tint**.

"What are you?" he asked without knowing where this strange animal had its beginning or its end. "What do you mean?" it boomed. "I am the giant amongst all creatures, and if you **tiny** animal keep your distance you will be able to see me better."

Zabu's head was ringing with this deep and loud voice. But he was much too curious to turn tail.

He only swam back a bit and then turned round full of **suspense**.

"Wow", he marvelled. "Unbelievable. You are a real giant!" What he saw in front of him was so huge it was hard to believe.

The mouth was similar to that of Ulina, the lady humpback whale, but much, much bigger. "Are you a giant humpback whale?" Zabu asked. "And could you do me a **favour**," he added quickly, "please, speak a bit more

quietly. My head hurts when you talk so loudly."

Zabu heard a rumbling laughter, but after that the giant did speak more quietly.

"I will try to lower my voice, my little friend. I am not a humpback whale, but you are not completely wrong. My kind also belongs to the baleen whales. I am a **blue whale** and my name is Makara."

Zabu introduced himself and then he asked the lady blue whale if he could swim all around her so he could admire her from all sides. Makara **had no objection to** this, but she made a **request**. "Could you do me a favour, please? There is something stuck in my back which **stings** terribly. Perhaps you could have a look at it."

"Of course, I'll do that", said Zabu and started to swim. The distance between Makara's head and her tail was so long that Zabu needed several strokes of his tail to cover it.

Makara was at least five times as long as Zabu, if not more. Zabu was particularly fascinated by her giant tail fin. Then he remembered Makara's request. He swam along the length of her back and investigated.

First he could not find anything, but then he discovered something. "Makara, I can see a kind of stick in your back. What happened?"

Makara sighed: "Quite some time ago I heard the noise of a ship. It came closer and closer, and when I surfaced full of curiosity, I was even able to see the people on this ship.

They were looking in my direction and I did not expect anything evil. But suddenly I saw this stick which they were throwing at me, and shortly afterwards I felt a sting in my back. It did not hurt badly but I dived to be safe.

I stayed under water for a long time, and when I had to surface to breathe, luckily the ship had disappeared. Since then I have been trying **to get rid of** this stick. Do you think you can manage to pull it out?"

Zabu had a closer look at the stick and tried to find out how deeply it was embedded in Makara's back and how he could best pull it out. "I don't want to hurt you, Makara," he sighed. "Don't worry, Zabu, it will only sting a bit. I have a thick layer of fat and hardly feel such injuries. There is no need to be afraid, you won't hurt me very much."

Zabu was relieved and started working immediately. He circled around the stick several times and then turned on his side to be able to grab the stick with his strong mouth and carefully started to pull.

"Ouch," Makara said, but Zabu pulled a bit more and then it was done. The stick was pulled out. It had a metal tip with two small **barbed hooks**.

Makara was relieved. "About time I got rid of this **annoying** thing. It had **bothered** me for a long time. Thanks a lot, Zabu." Zabu took the stick in his mouth and swam up to Makara's head. He showed the stick to her proudly and then let it sink into the depth of the ocean.

"Well done", Makara praised him, "perhaps I can also help you one day." – "Oh yes, thank you very much. All I want at the moment is to get back to my family from whom I was separated by a terrible net. Do you know where I can find them?"

Makara thought about this and then said: "If you swim towards the sunset you will meet some white whales. **Belugas** are always friendly and helpful. I am sure they will help you."

Zabu was grateful for this **advice**. He said good-bye to his giant friend and set out to find the white whales.

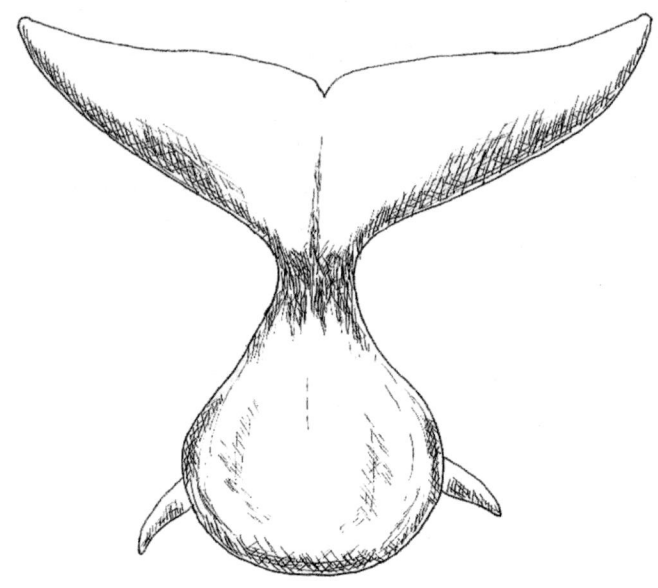

The Laughter of the Belugas

Zabu swam all evening. To stay his hunger he snapped up a few fish on the way and looked out for the white whales. After some time he was so tired that he had to rest for a while.

The sun was just setting. Zabu decided that he would not swim through the night, so he would not lose his way. He might pass the belugas without noticing them. So he stayed in one spot all night long. It was to be a very long night for Zabu.

It was completely dark around him, and when he surfaced to breathe, he could not even see the water glittering. Several times he thought he could see something, but when he looked closer, there was nothing. Zabu felt like he was being watched but no matter how hard he tried he could not discover anything. It was simply too dark. Again there was something. He could feel it **distinctly**. Right next to him. He turned around rapidly. Nothing.

This is how it went all night long. Zabu was extremely tired, but he could not sleep. Whenever he had become quiet, something roused him again. A spot of light. A strange noise.

When the sun finally rose, Zabu was completely **exhausted**. Once again he saw something, this time right in front of him. He thought he had been mistaken, but when daylight became brighter, Zabu could slowly distinguish a shape.

A white whale? As he was so tired, Zabu was not sure. Therefore, he gave a start when he was addressed suddenly: "No need to stare at me. I am not a ghost."

Zabu had to recover from his fright. "I really thought I was seeing ghosts. Did you also swim around me during the night?" he asked.

"Oh, yes," answered the white whale, "but not only I. My whole family had a lot of fun **teasing** you. It was so funny because you were so frightened." He giggled.

Zabu remembered how scared he had been and did not find this funny at all. But he remembered that he wanted some information from the white whales. He suppressed his anger even though he would have liked **to scold**.

The white whale realized this and continued in a friendly voice: "I hope you are not too mad at us. We were very curious but did not want to give ourselves away **initially**, because we did not know if you were dangerous. You look a lot like us, but you are black and a good deal bigger than we are and you have a mighty tail fin. What kind of a whale are you?"
"An orca," answered Zabu, "my name is Zabu."
– "My name is Gal," said the white whale.

The two of them circled each other for a while and watched each other full of curiosity.

"Well, look," Gal finally said, "you have quite a few white patches as well. Your belly is almost completely white. Perhaps you are as white as I am and we can rub away the black."

Zabu really did not think so, but Gal stuck to his opinion. Zabu became unsure of himself. Perhaps he really was a white whale?

Gal kept on at Zabu until the orca finally dived down to the bottom of the sea and rubbed his body on the ground. The sand scratched Zabu's skin when he tried to rub away the black.

"You see," he called out to Gal, "I am still black. I am not a white whale." Gal started giggling. Finally, he could no longer hold back. "**Had you**, had you," he snorted. "Pulled your leg!"

It dawned on Zabu that he had been fooled again. This time he should have known better. The trap he had fallen or rather swam into had been very **obvious**. Zabu had to laugh at himself. How stupid he had been. Little white Gal had taken him for a ride a second time.

Both whales laughed and fooled around happily for hours. Finally Zabu wanted to move on. He was afraid he might never see his family again. Makara had been right, the white whale was indeed able to give him a very accurate description of his route.

"Good luck for your search," he said. The beluga and the orca said good-bye, and when Zabu started swimming off he asked himself whether this had been his last adventure without his family.

Zabu swam in the direction indicated by the beluga. He caught a big fish for his dinner and when it became dark he was well-fed and extremely tired. The night before he had had little rest. As soon as the sun had set Zabu fell into a deep sleep from which he only awoke occasionally to draw breath.

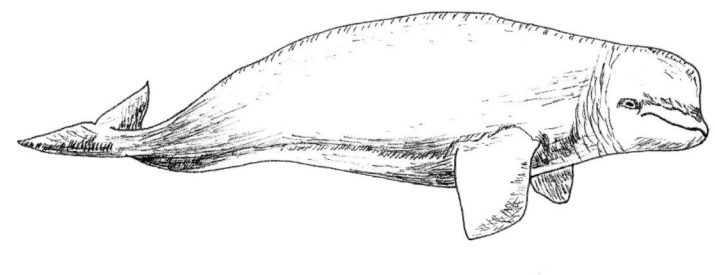

Dolphin Games

When the sun rose, Zabu was wide awake and set out quite happily. He was sure that he would find his family today.

With strong strokes of his tail fin he swam along. In between he had to surface to breathe, and he used these breaks to look around.

For quite a while there was nothing to be seen but the horizon and a calm sea. He swam and swam, and all the time he looked out for the big black **dorsal fins** of his family.

Finally he saw a dot on the horizon. He could not distinguish what it was and kept swimming towards it. He came closer very quickly and realized that it was a small boat.

To be on the safe side, Zabu dived like he had learned from his family. When he got closer to the boat he saw a whale that swam right next to the boat and jumped into the air from time to time. Full of curiosity, Zabu swam closer to the boat. He was supposed to keep away from boats, but the small grey whale did not seem to be in any danger. He jumped into the air in high spirits, made a few **somersaults** and splashed back into the water happily.

Zabu could not see much of the people in the boat. Something was dangling in the water. It was possibly a part of a human body, but Zabu was not sure. What use could such a strange part of a body be? How was he to know that he was seeing the legs of a person.

He switched his attention to the grey whale and admired his acrobatic stunts.

"Hello!" Zabu exclaimed. "Who are you and what are you doing there?" The small whale stopped his **romping** and made for Zabu like a flash of lightning.

"Hello, you lonesome orca. I am Bajashnoo, the dolphin. No need to remember this long name. I only need it when we meet another group of dolphins. From my name you can tell immediately which family of dolphins I belong to. Ba is the sign for our group, the extended family. Noo is my mother's name. You can call me Jash. Jash is really my name. And what's your name?"

Zabu told him and then asked once again: "What are you doing so close to the boat? Are you not afraid of humans?"

The dolphin was surprised: "Why should I be afraid of humans? They are always very friendly and sometimes they give me a few of the fish they have caught. The human in the boat is a small boy. We play together almost every day."

Zabu was amazed. In the past he had heard nothing but evil about humans and his own experiences had not been good so far.

Humans had separated him fom his family with a net and they had hurt the blue whale Makara with a stick. Were there really humans who were not dangerous and had no evil on their minds? Perhaps not all humans were bad.

"Come with me. There is no need to be afraid," Jash suggested and swam back to the little boat. Zabu **hesitated**, but then he followed the dolphin. Slowly and carefully he surfaced.

When he came to the surface and took a breath after ejecting a strong water fountain from his **blowhole**, he heard a shout from the boy in the boat. But Zabu could not understand human speech. Anyhow, the human did not look dangerous. He was only tiny.

The orca swam closer. Amazed, he watched the dolphin being touched by the boy. Then a red ball came flying from the boat.

Jash followed the ball and pushed it back to the boat with his long snout. The boy caught the ball and threw it again. And again the dolphin returned the ball. For a while this game went back and forth, and suddenly the ball was in front of Zabu. "Come on, play with us!" The dolphin shouted. "Why not," Zabu thought and touched the ball carefully.

It was smooth and light and Zabu was able to move it easily. Again and again he touched the ball with his forehead. Then he thought of something new. He dived underneath the ball, turned on his back, and when he was directly underneath the ball with his giant tail fin, he lifted his tail from the water very quickly and the ball flew high in the air.

The boy clapped his hands enthusiastically, and Jash, the dolphin, jumped out of the water with pleasure. Zabu enjoyed this new game. The boy fished the ball from the water and threw it again. Jash and Zabu started swimming at the same time to get to the red ball. This time the dolphin was first.

But Jash pushed the ball over to Zabu, and Zabu kicked it towards the boat with his tail fin again and again. Over and over again the red ball rushed through the air and both whales stormed after it. They played this game for quite a while.

Time passed quickly and midday came. The boy stopped throwing the ball.

He started a small engine and put-putted slowly towards the shore. Jash said good-bye to him by pushing his body far out of the water and showing his belly to the boy.

Zabu understood the sign and imitated the dolphin. "Today I have learned an important lesson," Zabu said, "humans can be friendly towards whales. This is great."

The dolphin agreed: "I told you so, but you didn't want to believe me. Tell me, what are you doing here all by yourself?"

Only now Zabu realized how much he missed his family. "Since you are asking," he said, "I am looking for my family. Gal, the beluga, described the way to me up to here. My family must be in the area somewhere. Any idea, where?" Jash gave the matter a quick thought: "No, I don't know, but one of my family is sure to know. Come on, we'll swim over to them. They are not far from here."

The dolphin swam ahead and Zabu had difficulties following him. Jash was so fast. They shot through the water at high speed and when they surfaced together to breathe, the water squirted to all sides.

It did not take very long and they saw a huge ship on the horizon. Zabu was afraid, but Jash kept swimming towards it with **undiminished** speed. By now Zabu trusted the dolphin and followed him. The ship's engines roared louder and louder. Soon they discovered Jash's family.

Zabu **twitched** and cried: "We must help them! Look, the ship is trying to run them over!" But Jash only laughed:

"It is only a game. They swim in front of the ship and let themselves be chased. It is great fun. You shouldn't try it, however. I am afraid, you are not quite fast enough." Zabu watched the dolphins jumping and romping in front of the big ship.

They shot through the water. "You are right, Jash. Unfortunately I am not as fast." Jash laughed again: "Just as well you accept it.

I will swim over and ask them if they know anything of the whereabouts of your family. Wait here for me."

He shot off. Zabu watched Jash joining the other dolphins for a short while.

He came straight back and informed Zabu: "Your family are not far from here. You can meet them today. If you swim in the direction which this ship came from you will meet your family soon. Best be off straight away, then you will find them before sunset. Take care, Zabu. We will surely meet again."

Zabu was very happy about this good news. "Thank you so much, Jash, my friend. See you soon." Zabu started swimming immediately. Then he hesitated and turned round. He saw the dolphin rising from the water with strong strokes of his tail. It was the sign for "good-bye". Zabu, too, lifted his great body vertically from the water surface to say good-bye. Then he continued his journey.

The Reunion

Impatiently he swam for a couple of hours. When the sun slowly started to set, he felt sad because he still had not found his family.

The sky turned red when the sun sent its last rays over the water. Suddenly, Zabu saw many big dorsal fins rising from the water like **sinister shades**. But these shades were familiar to him. They were his family! He had finally found them. His heart skipped a beat with happiness.

As fast as possible he swam towards them and shouted: "Mummy, Mummy! I'm back!" His family swam towards him enthusiastically and circled him while each of them touched him with their pectoral fins.

When they had all welcomed him, Zabu swam next to his mother happily. She touched him with her fins very softly. "I am so glad to be back with you," he said.

Zabu remembered all the exciting adventures of his journey. His family sensed this and they all became very curious.

"You won't believe what happened to me!" Zabu said and began telling his story.

Vocabulary

p. 7
ordinary	– gewöhnlich
orca	– Schwertwal
involuntary	– unfreiwillig

p. 8
to steer across	– hier: hinwegfahren über

p. 9
to rouse	– aufwecken
bewildered	– verwirrt
agitated	– aufgeregt

p. 11
to suffocate	– ersticken
to sob	– schluchzen
tail fin	– Schwanzflosse
death-trap	– tödliche Falle
to become entangled	– sich verfangen
impatient	– ungeduldig

p. 12
to surface	– auftauchen
to draw breath	– Luft holen
pectoral fin	– Brustflosse, Seitenflosse
to give sth. a wide berth	– einen großen Bogen um etw. machen

p. 15
predator	– Räuber
mammal	– Säugetier
seal	– Robbe

p. 16
jet of water	– Wasserstrahl
to swallow	– schlucken
to marvel	– staunen

p. 17
to be located	– liegen, sich befinden

p. 18
to be used to doing sth.	– es gewohnt sein, etw. zu tun
sperm whale	– Pottwal
indeed	– wirklich, tatsächlich
to flatter	– schmeicheln
to boast	– prahlen
octopus	– Krake

p. 19
incredulously	– ungläubig
suckers	– Saugnäpfe
feast	– Festmahl

p. 21
to admonish	– mahnen
squid	– Tintenfisch
to pounce upon	– sich stürzen auf

p. 22
shape	– Gestalt
to recover	– sich erholen

p. 23
prey	– Beute

p. 26
to distinguish	– klar erkennen
to moan	– jammern

p. 28
belly	– Bauch
humpback whale	– Buckelwal
baleen whale	– Bartenwal
sieve	– Sieb

p. 29
shark	– Hai

p. 30
to intervene	– eingreifen
at full tilt	– mit voller Wucht

p. 31		**p. 42**	
That showed him!	– Dem habe ich es aber gezeigt!	**exhausted**	– erschöpft
godmother	– Patentante	**p. 44**	
godfather	– Patenonkel	**to tease**	– necken
		to scold	– schimpfen
p. 32		**initially**	– anfangs
bent back	– gekrümmter Rücken		
relieved	– erleichtert	**p. 45**	
		Had you!	– Reingelegt!
p. 34		**p. 46**	
acquaintance	– Bekanntschaft	**obvious**	– offensichtlich
p. 35		**p. 49**	
vein	– hier: Ader	**dorsal fin**	– Rückenflosse
tint	– Farbton		
tiny	– winzig	**p. 50**	
suspense	– Spannung	**somersault**	– Salto
favour	– hier: Gefallen	**romping**	– Toberei
p. 36		**p. 52**	
blue whale	– Blauwal	**to hesitate**	– zögern
to have no objection to sth.	– nichts dagegen haben	**blowhole**	– Blasloch
request	– hier: Bitte	**p. 56**	
		undiminished	– unvermindert
p. 37		**to twitch**	– zusammenfahren, zusammenzucken
to sting	– stechen		
p. 38		**p. 59**	
to get rid of sth.	– etw. loswerden	**sinister**	– unheimlich
		shade	– Schatten
p. 39			
barbed hook	– Widerhaken		
to annoy so.	– jdn. nerven		
to bother	ärgern		
p. 40			
beluga	– Beluga, Weißwal		
advice	– Rat		
p. 41			
distinctly	– deutlich, klar		

Some interesting facts about whales

A whale is not a fish. Whales are mammals. They have warm blood like humans. To make sure they do not feel the cold in the water, whales have a thick layer of fat. In the case of the Greenland whale this layer of fat is 50 cm thick.

Whales must come to the water surface for breathing. They do not breathe through gills like fish, but they have lungs. When breathing out, the whale spurts the water which remains on the blowhole high into the air. Together with the condensated water of the warm breath this creates a jet of water. The blue whale's jet, also called blow, can be up to 9 meters high.

The baby whales grow in their mothers' bellies and are born live. They have to surface straight away after birth to draw breath. The mother whale suckles her baby for several years with a very fatty milk. Whales move their bodies up and down, which is typical for mammals, and not sideways like fish and reptiles. This is particularly obvious in the tail fin, the fluke.

A distinction is made between baleen whales and toothed whales. Toothed whales have up to 252 teeth and mostly feed on fish or squid. The orca also hunts seals in some areas and even attacks bigger whales. There are more than 70 different species of toothed whales.

The 11 species of baleen whales have a different method of feeding. They have frayed horn plates in their upper jaws which can be up to 4 meters long. They take tons of waters into their enormous mouths and filter it by pressing it through their baleens. The biggest baleen whale, the blue whale, feeds on the smallest animals in the sea, the plankton. Other types of baleen whales also feed on small kinds of fish.

The whale species appearing in this book:

Orca:	Toothed whale, up to 9 m long, dorsal fin up to 2 m
Sperm whale:	Toothed whale, up to 20 m long, can dive 3000 m deep and up to 2 hours
Humpback whale:	Baleen whale, up to 18 m long, well-known for its singing
Blue whale:	Baleen whale, up to 35 m long, weighs as much as 33 elephants
Beluga:	Toothed whale (white whale), up to 5.5 m long, weighs up to 1.4 tons
Dolphin:	Toothed whale, up to 4 m long, to be found in all oceans

Whale organisations

WDCS is the global voice for the protection of whales, dolphins and their environment. The organisation offers the chance to adopt an orca.
www.wdcs.org
info@wdcs.org

The Whale Museum
The Whale Museum is committed to providing a variety of education programs to share information on how we all can help the orcas. Adoptions help support this mission.
The Whale Museum
Friday Harbor
Washington/USA
www.whalemuseum.org

Wild Killer Whale
By becoming a member of the B.C. Wild Killer Whale Adoption Program you will be directly supporting research on wild killer whales.
B.C. Wild Killer Whale Adoption Program
Vancouver Aquarium Marine Science Centre
Vancouver
British Columbia/Canada
www.killerwhale.org

ORCALAB

OrcaLab
Homepage of Dr. Paul Spong and Helena Symonds who are doing research on the northern resident orcas in Johnstone Straight/Canada (shop with DVDs and CDs).
www.orcalab.org

Orca Live
Information about orcas, live sound, videos and community of the northern resident orcas.
www.orca-live.net

BornFree
Springer is an orphan orca. Sickly and alone, she was found swimming near Seattle/USA, but was identified by her calls. Springer was reunited with her family, the A4 orca pod, off the coast of British Columbia/Canada. Today the close-knit family feed, rest, play and travel together. (source: BornFree) www.bornfree.org.uk/give/adopt-an-animal/springer/

More about orcas (family structures, recorded calls): www.orcinusorca.nl